MW00654623

Presented to

Sis Salome Smalling

In appreciation for your service to the Lord

From

Heidelberg Gospel Service

Date

27 June 03

The heart of the giver makes
the gift dear and precious.

~Martin Luther

We always thank God for all of you,
mentioning you in our prayers.

1 Thessalonians 1:2

A Bushel Of Blessings for Teachers

In Celebration of Teachers

Christian Teacher's Aid

Providing Products To Help You Encourage God's People

A Bushel of Blessings

Compiled by: Cathy Varvaris
Contributions by: W. Michael Kilgore, Nancy Stallard, Todd Stallard, and Cathy Varvaris

Many customers tell us wonderful stories of how they use our products in their ministries. We have even had customers relate stories to us about how our products have actually started new ministries! If you have a story of how a CTA product has encouraged you or others, or how a product has been used, please let us know. Sharing your ideas and stories will encourage others and provide great new ideas for other churches!

To share stories please contact Customer Service at:

CTA
P.O. Box 1205
Fenton, MO 63026-1205

customerservice@CTAinc.com
1-800-999-1874

Printed in Thailand

Contents

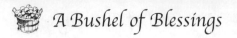

Planting

Scatter the seeds, and give them to God.
Dead they remain; til touched by his rod.
Each little seed is part of God's plan,
Maturing to fullness; blessed by his hand.
Scatter the seeds; place them not in soil,
But into God's palm, let him work and toil.
Be there to bless them, and meet all their needs,
God's grace will rain down; just scatter the seeds.

1

Planting the Seeds

Again he said, "What shall we say the kingdom of God is like, or what parable shall we use to describe it? It is like a mustard seed, which is the smallest seed you plant in the ground. Yet when planted, it grows and becomes the largest of all garden plants, with such big branches that the birds of the air can perch in its shade."

Mark 4:30-32

Not just part of us becomes a teacher. It engages the whole self – the woman or man, wife or husband, mother or father, the lover, scholar or artist in you as well as the teacher earning money.   ~Sylvia Ashton-Warner

Show me your ways, O Lord, teach me your paths; guide me in your truth and teach me, for you are God my Savior, and my hope is in you all day long.

Psalm 25:4-5

...Let the little children come to me, and do not hinder them, for the kingdom of God belongs to such as these. Mark 10:14

The greatest natural resource that any country can have is its children.   ~Danny Kaye

Lord, thank you for the children you have put in my life. Guide and teach me as I teach them. Let me see them through your loving eyes. Kindle the flames of my faith so I can trust you to provide all I need, for what you have called me to do.

And Some to Be Teachers...

It was he who gave some to be apostles, some to be prophets, some to be evangelists, and some to be pastors and teachers, to prepare God's people for works of service, so that the body of Christ may be built up Ephesians 4:11-12

We've all been given certain gifts
He wants us to use well.
It's clear to see the gift to teach
Within you deep does dwell

And as we see you use that gift
In classrooms every day,
Your love of teaching radiates
Through all you do and say.

This precious gift of God is giv'n
To only just a few.
We're daily blessed to feel His love
Shining brightly through you!

Those who sow in tears will reap with songs of joy.　　Psalm 126:5

A plant cannot be grown
Unless a seed is thrown.
A flower cannot sprout
If water's not about.
A tree cannot bear fruit
Without a long, strong root.
A tree will reach no height
When kept from sun's rich light.
A plant cannot be grown
Unless a seed is thrown.

Lord, thank you for the gifts you have given me. Remind me that who I am is much more important than what I teach. Give me joy as I serve and help me to be a blessing to others.

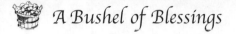

A Teacher's ABC'S

Although things are not perfect
Because of trial or pain,
Continue in thanksgiving;
Do not begin to blame.
Even when times are hard, and
Fierce winds begin to blow,
God is forever able—
Hold on to what you know.
Imagine life without God's love:
Joy would cease to be.
Keep thanking him for all the things
Love imparts to thee.
Move out of "Camp Complaining";
No weapon that is known
On earth can yield the power
Praise can do alone.
Quit looking at the future,
Redeem the time at hand.
Start every day with worship—
To thank is a command!
Until we see him coming
Victorious in the sky,
We'll run the race with gratitude
Xalting God most high.
Yes, there'll be good times, and yes, some will be bad, but...
Zion waits in glory . . . where none are ever sad!

~Author Unknown

The future of the nation is on the shoulders of teachers and how they teach kids; the future of the world is in the classroom where the teachers are. ~Richard Reginald Green

Teach me, O Lord, to follow your decrees; then I will keep them to the end. Psalm 119:33

A farmer went out to sow his seed...
Matthew 13:3

The Parable of the Sower

Each year a teacher plans to sow,
Not knowing how the seeds will grow.
Some seeds are eaten from the road,
But the teacher's work won't be slowed.
Some other seeds find lifeless soil.
Still hopefully the teacher toils.
The sun destroys the rootless seeds
And some are choked by thorns and weeds.
Still the teacher sows, though some fall
Upon good soil and start out small.
Then while they grow the teacher cares,
Supports, uplifts, guides and prepares.
God takes the seeds the teacher sowed,
Increasing them a hundred fold!

Preach the Word; be prepared in season and out of season; correct, rebuke and encourage - with great patience and careful instruction.   2 Timothy 4:2

Self-sacrifice is the real miracle out of which all the reported miracles grow.   ~Ralph Waldo Emerson

Thank you, Father, for the teachers who continue to sow seeds in your name. Give them the faith to trust you for the results of their labor. Allow them to see growth in their students so that they will be encouraged.

In the Middle of a Long, Dull Stretch

Father,
I confess that the prospect of another day
Stretching before me
Is a burden,
Rather than a joy.
Refresh me, Father.
Ease the tension that comes from boredom.
Show me how to bring vitality to a job that's gone stale.
Restore to me the absorbing joy of an artist at work,
For truly good teaching is an art.
Oh, Father,
You have given me time,
And you have given me skill.
Teach me to take delight in both,
Using my time and my skill
To do something worthwhile,
To teach.

Elspeth Campbell Murphy

Peacemakers who sow in peace raise a harvest of righteousness.   James 3:18

The Prayer of St. Francis of Assisi

Lord, make me an instrument of Thy peace.
    Where there is hatred, let me sow love.
    Where there is injury, pardon.
    Where there is doubt, faith.
    Where there is despair, hope.
    Where there is darkness, light.
    Where there is sadness, joy.

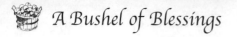

Nurturing

Father, help me love my students
The way that you've loved me.
Sometimes there is pruning
And your hand seems rather harsh,
But other times you're tender
You hope to see new growth.
For now I'm praying day and night
That I will love my students
The way that you've loved me.

2

Nurturing the Seedling

Whatever you do, work at it with all your heart, as working for the Lord, not for men, since you know that you will receive an inheritance from the Lord as a reward. It is the Lord Christ you are serving.
Colossians 3:23-24

19

Their Eyes
Are Watching You

So much to discover,
So much that is new,
Will truth and love shine from your face?
Their eyes are watching you.

You're blessed with a calling,
To fill hearts in need;
Those hearts have grown since yesterday,
When first you sowed the seed.

These souls are your work field,
They're young, pure, and true,
Will you both love and nurture them?
Their eyes are always watching you!

The curriculum is so much neces-
sary raw material, but warmth is
the vital element for the growing
plant and for the soul of the child.

~Carl Jung

*Father, guard my mouth that I may only
speak encouraging words to my students.
Guide my actions so that they will always
reflect you. Remind me that their little
eyes are always watching me. Help me to
be an example to them that is worthy of
imitating. Give me your love for these
precious children.*

*There is no such whetstone,
to sharpen a good wit and
encourage a will to learning,
as is praise.* ~Roger Ascham

In Praise of Children

Lord, you have made these children
As varied as the flowers of a garden.
You have blessed each one uniquely.
And each fragile, growing child
Is infinitely precious in your sight.
You have trusted me to nurture them.
And blessed me with the joy of
Seeing them grow.
Lord, I teach in reverence.

~Elspeth Campbell Murphy

Nurturing

Say a prayer for the students
That you teach today;
That God will take the seeds you plant,
And make them grow His way.

Say a prayer that their hearts will
Send roots ever deep;
That fed by Living Water they
Will want God's Word to keep.

That nurtured by the wisdom
Your heart shows these seeds;
They'll prosper and grow strong and true,
And bear much fruit indeed.

*He is like a tree planted by streams of
water, which yields its fruit in season
and whose leaf does not wither...*

Psalm 1:3

In teaching, and almost any other profession, they won't care how much you know until they know how much you care.

~Anonymous

Trust in the Lord with all your heart and lean not on your own understanding; in all your ways acknowledge him, and he will make your paths straight. Proverbs 3:5-6

We should not be speaking to, but with. That is second nature to any good teacher.

~Noam Chomsky

The Tone of Voice

It's not so much what we say
As the manner in which we say it.
It's not so much the language we use
As the tone in which we convey it.
      "Come here," I sharply ordered;
And a child cowered and wept.
      "Come here," I softly whispered;
And into my arms he crept.
Words may be mild and fair,
But the tone pierces like a dart.
Words may be soft as summer air,
But the tone can break a heart.

                              ~Author Unknown

Lord, it is so easy to lose my temper when I am stressed and exhausted. Let my voice reflect a genuine spirit which is not dependent on my own circumstances. Help me to model the unconditional love and acceptance that you always give to me.

At the End of A Good Day

Father,
Today I felt your presence
In the classroom.
By faith I know that you are always there,
But thank you for those times which confirm
That in you we live
And move
And have our being.

Father,
Today it all felt so right.
The children were joyously absorbed
In what they were learning,
And I moved among them
Full of the satisfaction of a job well done.
Thank you for those times of quiet joy
When it is good
Just to be.
Thank you for gently reminding me
That you have brought the children and me
Together for a purpose,
And that the work you have given me to do
Is a sacred trust.   Elpspeth Campbell Murphy

*A word aptly spoken is like apples of
gold in settings of silver.*　　Proverbs 25:11

A million words or more to us
You certainly had said.
Day after day we listened as
You taught, explained and read.

But one small, simple phrase stands out
From all the rest.
I heard you share it often while
I struggled at my desk.

When words or numbers jumbled and
I couldn't understand,
You shared the might of two small words
The little giants "I Can!"

Education consists of example and love- nothing else.

~Heinrich Pestalozzi

Teach me to do your will, for you are my God; may your good Spirit lead me on level ground.   Psalm 143:10

Educators should be chosen not merely for their special qualifications, but more for their personality and their character, because we teach more by what we are than by what we teach.

~Will Durant

At its heart, teaching includes concern for both content and relationships, for both knowing and becoming. Teachers care about imparting information and inspiring transformation in students' hearts. ~Jane L. Fryar

I urge you ... in view of God's mercy, to offer yourselves as living sacrifices, holy and pleasing to God—which is your spiritual worship. Do not conform any longer to the pattern of this world, but be transformed by the renewing of your mind .... Romans 12:1-2

Harvest

Will you join in the harvest now?
See all he's done in them through you!
View blessings galore,
From seeds thrown before,
The harvest, at last, has come through!

Won't you join in the harvest now?
Though some seed may never have grown,
So many he's blessed
As you did your very best.
Come harvest the seeds you have sown!

3

Gathering the Harvest

...I tell you, open your eyes and look at the fields! They are ripe for harvest. Even now the reaper draws his wages, even now he harvests the crop for eternal life, so that the sower and the reaper may be glad together.   John 4:35-36

Tiny seeds
Fertile soil
Sun
+ Rain
_____
Harvest

Let us not become weary in doing good,
for at the proper time we will reap a
harvest if we do not give up.

Galatians 6:9

For Consistency

Father, you who are the same
yesterday,
today,
and forever,
help me to be consistent.

Help me to make my classroom a secure and
stable place,
where the children know what I expect of them;
and what they can expect from me.
I pray that it might be said of my classroom that
nothing was ever promised that was not given,
nothing was ever threatened that was not
carried out,
nothing was ever said that was not true,
nothing was ever taught that had to be
unlearned.

Elspeth Campbell Murphy

Teacher

Taking the time

Every day, to

Affirm them

Care for them, and

Help each student,

Expecting them to learn, so they can

Reach others for You!

...know that your labor in the Lord is not in vain.   1 Corinthians 15:58

Your Harvest

Some days it's very hard
To plant and nurture seeds.
Will harvest ever come
Through all your work and deeds?

The Father's watchful eye
Observes all you've planted.
Be patient and you'll see
Rich harvests He's granted!

Amazingly, the crops
Yield more than you had dreamed.
Keep sowing seeds on earth;
In heav'n the gain you'll see!

A teacher affects eternity; no one can tell where his influence stops.   ~Henry Adams

Now he who supplies seed to the sower and bread for food will also supply and increase your store of seed and will enlarge the harvest of your righteousness.   2 Corinthians 9:10

Lord, I often forget that you go on working long after my lessons are over. Help me to trust you for the harvest. I entrust my students into your loving care, for I know that you love them even more than I do!

They are Destined to Gain

Your work is not in vain;
The minds you hope to train.
Your work is not for naught;
Attempts to mold each thought.
Your efforts reap one day;
Success that comes their way.
They'll see the love you gave,
The paths your lessons paved.
Your work is not in vain;
Bright futures they will gain.

Give, and it will be given to you. A good measure, pressed down, shaken together and running over, will be poured into your lap. For with the measure you use, it will be measured to you. Luke 6:38

Six days you shall labor, but on the seventh day you shall rest; even during the plowing season and harvest you must rest.

Exodus 34:21

Finish every day and be done
  with it.
You have done what you could...
Tomorrow is a new day.

~Ralph Waldo Emerson

And we pray...that you may live a life worthy of the Lord and may please him in every way: bearing fruit in every good work, growing in the knowledge of God, being strengthened with all power according to his glorious might...

Colossians 1:10-11

I thank my God every time I remember you.
... being confident of this, that he who
began a good work in you will carry it on
to completion until the day of Christ Jesus.
Philippians 1:3,6

Lord, bless this teacher who has blessed
so many students by their years of
service for you. Meet every need they
have. Guard and protect them from the
enemy who would seek to destroy their
spirit. Daily give them your strength and
fill them with your Holy Spirit. Let them
see their students through your eyes of
love. Remind them to keep sowing seeds
of love and to nurture those you have
placed in their care. Bless the work of
their hands with a mighty harvest that
will glorify you!

We thank You...

We thank you,
for the hours you spend preparing,
the many days you spend planting,
the tender souls you nurture so carefully,
and the harvest that's been produced so wonderfully...

Our school would not be the same
without your hard work and dedication,
your smiles and enthusiasm,
your love for God and each student here,
your tireless effort and the way you care...

We can only pray that God above
      showers you with

A Bushel of Blessings and Love!